TABEL OF CONTENTS

*TELL ME YOUR LIFE
STORY*

Dear grandmother

I'll give you this diary so that you can make me the most Beautiful gift: the gift of your story and life experience. I know and love the person you are through today Your role as grandmother, but I would also like to discover your Other facets and the different phases that have marked your Existence and that have made you the woman you are today. You just have to give me back this diary completed with your thoughts, Anecdotes and the most personal memories. You can either the Fill it with me, or do it on your side. Don't feel obliged to answer each of the questions if you Don't feel like it. They have been designed to guide your Life testimony and can be supplemented by your own Reflections at the end of the newspaper and embellished with your most beautiful Photos! Once you have finished your story, I will keep Preciously this souvenir book, an invaluable treasure that can Be passed on to my descendants.

I hope you will enjoy filling it as much as I do Will have to read it.

Thank you very much

My Details

Full name :

Date of birth :

Place of birth :

Eye color :

Height :

Hair coclor :

Distinguishing marks :

Attach your baby photo here

Time capsule

Today's date :

Population of your city :

Population of your country :

Leader of your country :

Tell Me About YOU

My childrens

FIRST NAME

LAST NAME & MAIDEN NAME

DATE OF BIRTH	BIRTH PLACE
EYE COLOR	HAIR COLOR

OCCUPATION

FIRST NAME

LAST NAME & MAIDEN NAME

DATE OF BIRTH	BIRTH PLACE
EYE COLOR	HAIR COLOR

OCCUPATION

FIRST NAME

LAST NAME & MAIDEN NAME

DATE OF BIRTH	BIRTH PLACE
EYE COLOR	HAIR COLOR

OCCUPATION

FIRST NAME

LAST NAME & MAIDEN NAME

DATE OF BIRTH	BIRTH PLACE
EYE COLOR	HAIR COLOR

OCCUPATION

My siblings

FIRST NAME

LAST NAME & MAIDEN NAME

DATE OF BIRTH	BIRTH PLACE
EYE COLOR	HAIR COLOR

OCCUPATION

FIRST NAME

LAST NAME & MAIDEN NAME

DATE OF BIRTH	BIRTH PLACE
EYE COLOR	HAIR COLOR

OCCUPATION

FIRST NAME

LAST NAME & MAIDEN NAME

DATE OF BIRTH	BIRTH PLACE
EYE COLOR	HAIR COLOR

OCCUPATION

FIRST NAME

LAST NAME & MAIDEN NAME

DATE OF BIRTH	BIRTH PLACE
EYE COLOR	HAIR COLOR

OCCUPATION

My parents

FIRST NAME

LAST NAME & MAIDEN NAME

DATE OF BIRTH	BIRTH PLACE
EYE COLOR	HAIR COLOR

OCCUPATION

FIRST NAME

LAST NAME & MAIDEN NAME

DATE OF BIRTH	BIRTH PLACE
EYE COLOR	HAIR COLOR

OCCUPATION

FIRST NAME

LAST NAME & MAIDEN NAME

DATE OF BIRTH	BIRTH PLACE
EYE COLOR	HAIR COLOR

OCCUPATION

FIRST NAME

LAST NAME & MAIDEN NAME

DATE OF BIRTH	BIRTH PLACE
EYE COLOR	HAIR COLOR

OCCUPATION

My grandchildren

FIRST NAME

LAST NAME & MAIDEN NAME

DATE OF BIRTH	BIRTH PLACE
EYE COLOR	HAIR COLOR

OCCUPATION

FIRST NAME

LAST NAME & MAIDEN NAME

DATE OF BIRTH	BIRTH PLACE
EYE COLOR	HAIR COLOR

OCCUPATION

FIRST NAME

LAST NAME & MAIDEN NAME

DATE OF BIRTH	BIRTH PLACE
EYE COLOR	HAIR COLOR

OCCUPATION

FIRST NAME

LAST NAME & MAIDEN NAME

DATE OF BIRTH	BIRTH PLACE
EYE COLOR	HAIR COLOR

OCCUPATION

My grandparents

FIRST NAME

LAST NAME & MAIDEN NAME

DATE OF BIRTH	BIRTH PLACE
EYE COLOR	HAIR COLOR

OCCUPATION

FIRST NAME

LAST NAME & MAIDEN NAME

DATE OF BIRTH	BIRTH PLACE
EYE COLOR	HAIR COLOR

OCCUPATION

Your Roots

Your most beautiful photo

Does your name have a special meaning? If so, what does it mean?

_____
_____
_____
_____
_____
_____
_____
_____
_____
_____
_____
_____
_____
_____

How many siblings do you have and which birth order are you in your family?

_____
_____
_____
_____
_____
_____
_____
_____
_____
_____
_____
_____
_____
_____

Does your name have a special meaning? If so, what does it mean?

_____
_____
_____
_____
_____
_____
_____
_____
_____
_____
_____
_____
_____

How many siblings do you have and which birth order are you in your family?

_____
_____
_____
_____
_____
_____
_____
_____
_____
_____
_____
_____

What did you name your first doll, stuffed animal, or special blanket? Describe what it/they looked like.

What type of clothes did you like to wear when you were a teen? Describe your favorite outfit(s).

What were some typical family meals? Which one did you most look forward to?

As a child, who were you told you resembled, if anyone?

_____
_____
_____
_____
_____
_____
_____
_____
_____
_____
_____
_____
_____
_____

*Aside from your parents, which relatives do you remember
being around   when you were a child and what do you
remember about them?*

_____
_____
_____
_____
_____
_____
_____
_____
_____
_____
_____
_____
_____
_____

Did your parents make time to play games or do activities with you? What memories stand out?

_____
_____
_____
_____
_____
_____
_____
_____
_____
_____
_____
_____

Were you encouraged to save money as a child, or were you free to spend it on anything you liked?

_____
_____
_____
_____
_____
_____
_____
_____
_____
_____
_____
_____

What schoolyard games or trends were popular when you were growing up? What was the "in thing" for kids at the time?

When you were little, what did you dream of being when you grew up and who encouraged you to believe in your dreams?

_____
_____
_____
_____
_____
_____
_____
_____
_____
_____
_____
_____
_____

Did your parents want you to pursue a certain profession or job? If so, what, and why?

_____
_____
_____
_____
_____
_____
_____
_____
_____
_____
_____
_____

Was there something that you were the first to do in your family? Was it a big deal at the time?

_____
_____
_____
_____
_____
_____
_____
_____
_____
_____
_____
_____

How old were you when you first left home permanently? How did you feel on the day you left?

_____
_____
_____
_____
_____
_____
_____
_____
_____
_____
_____
_____

Are there leisure activities you used to spend a lot of time doing that you no longer do? What changed?

_____
_____
_____
_____
_____
_____
_____
_____
_____
_____
_____
_____
_____

What do you look forward to doing in your later years or when you retire?

_____
_____
_____
_____
_____
_____
_____
_____
_____
_____
_____
_____
_____

What was your parents' relationship like with their parents (your grandparents)?

_____

_____

_____

_____

_____

_____

_____

_____

_____

_____

_____

_____

_____

What behaviors do you see in yourself that you also see (or saw) in your grandparents?

_____

_____

_____

_____

_____

_____

_____

_____

_____

_____

_____

_____

Thinking of all your ancestors whom you never knew, which one would you most like to meet and why?

_____
_____
_____
_____
_____
_____
_____
_____
_____
_____
_____

Did you have a favorite or least favorite aunt, uncle, or cousin? What stories can you tell about them?

_____
_____
_____
_____
_____
_____
_____
_____
_____
_____
_____

How did you know when you were in love?

What milestone of child rearing were you excited to reach?

_____
_____
_____
_____
_____
_____
_____
_____
_____
_____
_____

Is there one piece of parenting advice you received that you feel strongly about passing on down through every new generation of parents in your family?

_____
_____
_____
_____
_____
_____
_____
_____
_____
_____
_____
_____

Who was the first person you told you were
going to be a parent or grandparent?

Were there any "I'm turning into my parents" moments in your
parenthood journey, or moments when you realized you were
more like your parents than you thought?

What is your favorite memory about parenthood in general?

How old were you when you voted for the first time?

Who is or was the best president or prime minister of your lifetime?

Do you think it's ok to tell a lie? Why or why not?

_____
_____
_____
_____
_____
_____
_____
_____
_____
_____
_____

What role does religion have in your life?

_____
_____
_____
_____
_____
_____
_____
_____
_____
_____
_____
_____
_____

Do you believe in miracles? Have you ever experienced a miracle? If so, what was it?

What are you grateful for?

_____

_____

_____

_____

_____

_____

_____

_____

_____

_____

_____

_____

_____

What can you do better than anyone else in the family?

_____

_____

_____

_____

_____

_____

_____

_____

_____

_____

_____

_____

_____

Was having a family as rewarding as you thought it would be?

Is there any area of your life you neglected that you wish you hadn't? If so, what is it?

What was the hardest lesson for you to learn as you grew up?

_____

_____

_____

_____

_____

_____

_____

_____

_____

_____

_____

_____

What family traditions do you hope to pass down and why?

_____

_____

_____

_____

_____

_____

_____

_____

_____

_____

_____

_____

What is something you're proud of that nobody would know about?

_____
_____
_____
_____
_____
_____
_____
_____
_____
_____
_____
_____
_____

Has there been an event that has changed the course of your life? If so, explain it.

_____
_____
_____
_____
_____
_____
_____
_____
_____
_____
_____
_____
_____

Describe a time when you had to show courage.

_____

_____

_____

_____

_____

_____

_____

_____

_____

_____

_____

_____

*Have you ever taken a stand against what your friends or family
wanted to do, or did you follow the crowd? Looking back, what
would you have done differently, if anything?*

_____

_____

_____

_____

_____

_____

_____

_____

_____

_____

_____

Have you ever wanted to have your own business?
If so, what kind of business would it be?

_____
_____
_____
_____
_____
_____
_____
_____
_____
_____
_____
_____
_____

Do you think there is a secret or key to happiness? If so, what is
it?

_____
_____
_____
_____
_____
_____
_____
_____
_____
_____
_____
_____
_____

What is something your parents taught you that you didn't
fully understand or appreciate until you were an adult?

What is a mistake you made that never want your children to
repeat?

What important lessons you've learned about relationships?

Things to be thankful for in life

1.
2.
3.
4.
5.

Activities on your bucket list

1.
2.
3.
4.
5.

"Essential" items that you always have in your purse or pockets

1.
2.
3.
4.
5.

Most memorable restaurant meals

1.
2.
3.
4.
5.

Pet peeves

1.
2.
3.
4.
5.

Phobias or irrational fears

1.
2.
3.
4.
5.

Biggest adventures in life so far

1.
2.
3.
4.
5.

Items on your "Things I Will NEVER Do" list

1.
2.
3.
4.
5.

Do you share a birthday with anyone famous?

_____

_____

_____

Would you describe yourself as a leader or a follower?

_____

_____

_____

If you could have dinner with anyone in the world, living or dead,
who would it be and why?

_____

_____

_____

What TV shows did you watch most when you were a kid?

_____

_____

_____

What candy bar did you love as a child?

_____

_____

_____

How many of your childhood/school friends are you still in
contact with?

_____

_____

_____

Do you believe in ghosts?

Have you ever had a "supernatural" experience, or an experience you couldn't explain?

Have you ever been told you look like someone famous? If so, who?

What type of chocolate do you always pick out of the box first?

What have you done in life that you said you would never do?

What are your thoughts on reincarnation?

What is the most dangerous thing you have ever done?

Have you ever wished on a star and had the wish come true?

What one change would you like to make to the law?

Do you read your horoscope? Do you ever believe it?

Which famous people did you have a crush on when you were growing up?

Is there something you have secretly always wanted to do that might surprise people?

Is there something you always wanted as a child but didn't get until you were an adult?

Have you ever made the same mistake twice? If so, what was it?

What is one of the bravest things you've ever had to do?

♥ Notes ♥

YOUR HOPES

Attach your family photo here

Made in the USA
Monee, IL
06 April 2022

94207558R10030